TABLE OF CONTENTS

ROUND 1

Monster Jokes

WHY DID THE BIG HAIRY, MONSTER GIVE UP BOXING?

BECAUSE HE DIDN'T WANT TO SPOIL HIS LOOKS.

WHAT IS BIG HAIRY AND BOUNCES UP AND DOWN?

A MONSTER ON A POGO STICK!

ROUND 1 : MONSTER JOKES

HOW DOES FRANKENSTEIN GET AROUND TOWN?

MONSTER TRUCK!

WHY COULDN'T THE GHOST SEE ITS MOM AND DAD?

BECAUSE THEY WERE TRANS-PARENTS!

WHEN DO GHOSTS USUALLY APPEAR?
JUST BEFORE SOMEONE SCREAMS!

WHY ARE VAMPIRES SO EASY TO FOOL?
BECAUSE THEY ARE SUCKERS.

ROUND 1 : MONSTER JOKES

WHAT GOES AROUND A HAUNTED HOUSE AND NEVER STOPS?
A FENCE!

WHAT DO YOU GET WHEN YOU CROSS A WEREWOLF WITH A HYENA?
A MONSTER WITH A SENSE OF HUMOR!

WHAT DO VAMPIRES TAKE WHEN THEY ARE SICK?

COFFIN DROPS!

HOW CAN YOU TELL A VAMPIRE LIKES BASEBALL?

EVERY NIGHT HE TURNS INTO A BAT.

ROUND 1 : MONSTER JOKES

HOW DO YOU STOP A MONSTER FROM SMELLING?

CUT OFF HIS NOSE!

WHAT DO YOU CALL A SMART MONSTER?

FRANK EINSTEIN!

WHY COULDN'T THE SKELETON SKYDIVE?
HE DIDN'T HAVE THE GUTS!

WHAT DID THE WEREWOLF SAY TO THE FLEA?
STOP BUGGING ME!

ROUND 1 : MONSTER JOKES

WHAT DID THE MONSTER DO WHEN HE LOST A HAND?
HE WENT TO THE SECOND-HAND SHOP!

WHY DO WITCHES FLY ON BROOMS?
VACUUM CLEANER CORDS ARE TOO SHORT.

HOW CAN YOU TELL IF A MONSTER HAS A GLASS EYE?

IT COMES OUT IN A CONVERSATION!

WHY DOESN'T FRANKENSTEIN GO ON AIRPLANES?

HE CAN'T GET PAST THE AIRPORT METAL DETECTOR.

ROUND 1 : MONSTER JOKES

WHAT DO YOU CALL A ZOMBIE WHO KEEPS PRESSING YOUR DOORBELL?

A DEAD RINGER!

WHAT DO YOU DO IF YOU SEE ZOMBIES AROUND YOUR HOUSE?

HOPE IT'S HALLOWEEN!

WHY ARE GHOSTS BAD LIARS?
YOU CAN SEE RIGHT THROUGH THEM.

WHAT KIND OF GHOST HAS THE BEST HEARING?
THE EERIEST!

ROUND 1 : MONSTER JOKES

WHAT DOES MONSTER DO WHEN HE LOSES HIS HEAD?
HE CALLS THE HEAD-HUNTER!

DO ZOMBIES EAT POPCORN WITH THEIR FINGERS?
NO, THEY EAT THEIR FINGERS SEPARATELY.

WHAT'S THE PROBLEM WITH TWIN WITCHES?
YOU CAN'T TELL WHICH WITCH IS WHICH!

WHERE DO ZOMBIES LIVE?
ON DEAD END STREETS.

ROUND 1 : MONSTER JOKES

WHY DIDN'T THE SKELETON EAT SPICY FOOD?
HE DIDN'T HAVE THE STOMACH FOR IT.

WHAT BREED OF DOG DOES DRACULA HAVE?
A BLOODHOUND!

WHY WAS FRANKENSTEIN'S MONSTER IN JAIL?
HE COULDN'T DENY THE CHARGE.

WHAT KIND OF DESSERT DO ZOMBIES LIKE?
I-SCREAM!

ROUND 1 : MONSTER JOKES

WHY DO GHOSTS ONLY EAT VEGETABLES?
BECAUSE IT'S SUPER-NATURAL.

WHAT TYPE OF ARTIST WAS THE SKELETON?
A SKULLPTOR.

WHAT HAPPENED WHEN THE WEREWOLF WENT TO THE FLEA CIRCUS?

HE STOLE THE SHOW!

WHAT KIND OF MONSTER CAN SIT ON THE END OF YOUR FINGER?

THE BOGEYMAN!

ROUND 1 : MONSTER JOKES

WHAT KIND OF MUSIC DOES A MUMMY LISTEN TO ON HIS I-POD?

WRAP.

WHAT DOES A SKELETON ORDER WHEN HE GOES TO A BAR?

A BEER AND A MOP.

ROUND 2

Animal

Jokes

WHY DO GIRAFFES HAVE LONG NECKS?
BECAUSE THEY HAVE STINKY FEET!

WHY IS THE BARN SO NOISY?
BECAUSE THE COWS HAVE HORNS!

ROUND 2 : ANIMAL JOKES

WHAT'S SMALL, FURRY AND BRIGHT PURPLE?
A KOALA HOLDING ITS BREATH!

WHY DID THE FISH BLUSH?
BECAUSE IT SAW THE OCEANS BOTTOM!

WHY DO CATS MAKE TERRIBLE STORYTELLERS?

BECAUSE THEY ONLY HAVE ONE TAIL.

WHY DO PANDAS LIKE OLD MOVIES?

BECAUSE THEY ARE BLACK AND WHITE!

ROUND 2 : ANIMAL JOKES

WHY DO GORILLAS HAVE BIG NOSTRILS?

BECAUSE THEY HAVE BIG FINGERS!

WHY DO PENGUINS CARRY FISH IN THEIR BEAKS?

BECAUSE THEY DON'T HAVE ANY POCKETS!

WHAT GOES "HUM-CHOO, HUM-CHOO"?
A BEE WITH A COLD!

WHEN IS TURKEY SOUP BAD FOR YOUR HEALTH?
WHEN YOU'RE THE TURKEY!

ROUND 2 : ANIMAL JOKES

WHY DID THE LION SPIT OUT THE CLOWN?
BECAUSE HE TASTED FUNNY!

WHAT DO YOU CALL AN ALLIGATOR IN A VEST?
INVESTIGATOR!

WHY FROGS ARE SO HAPPY?
THEY EAT WHATEVER BUGS THEM.

WHAT DO YOU CALL A PONY WITH A COUGH?
A LITTLE HOARSE.

ROUND 2 : ANIMAL JOKES

WHAT DO YOU CALL A WOODPECKER WITH NO BEAK?
A HEADBANGER!

WHAT HAS 50 LEGS BUT CAN'T WALK?
HALF A CENTIPEDE!

WHAT HAPPENED TO THE CAT THAT SWALLOWED A BALL OF WOOL?

SHE HAD MITTENS!

WHY COULDN'T THE LEOPARD EVER ESCAPE FROM THE ZOO?

HE WAS ALWAYS SPOTTED!

ROUND 2 : ANIMAL JOKES

WHEN IS IT BAD LUCK TO SEE A BLACK CAT?

WHEN YOU'RE A MOUSE!

WHAT A DOG WILL DO WHEN HE LOSES HIS TAIL?

HE WILL PREFER TO GO TO A RE-TAIL STORE.

WHAT STEPS WILL YOU TAKE IF A BEAR IS RUNNING TOWARDS YOU?

BIG ONES!

WHAT DO YOU GET IF YOU CROSS A CANARY AND A 50-FOOT LONG SNAKE?

A SING-A-LONG!

ROUND 2 : ANIMAL JOKES

HOW DO YOU KNOW IF THERE'S A DINOSAUR HIDING UNDER YOUR BED?

YOUR NOSE HITS THE CEILING!

WHAT DO YOU GET WHEN YOU CROSS A SNAKE AND A PIE?

A PIE-THON!

WHAT KIND OF KEY OPENS A BANANA?
A MON-KEY!

WHY WAS THE CAT SCARED OF THE TREE?
BECAUSE OF ITS BARK!

ROUND 2 : ANIMAL JOKES

WHY ARE ELEPHANTS SO WRINKLED?
BECAUSE IT WILL TAKE TOO LONG TO IRON AN ELEPHANT!

WHY DO HUMMINGBIRDS HUM?
BECAUSE THEY DON'T KNOW THE WORDS!

WHAT DO YOU GIVE AN ELEPHANT WITH BIG FEET?
PLENTY OF ROOM!

WHY IS THERE A CRAB IN PRISON?
BECAUSE HE KEPT PINCHING THINGS!

ROUND 2 : ANIMAL JOKES

WHAT ANIMAL IS BEST AT BASEBALL?
A BAT!

WHY DID THE SPARROW GO TO THE LIBRARY?
IT WAS LOOKING FOR BOOKWORMS.

WHY ARE CATS SO GOOD AT VIDEO GAMES?
BECAUSE THEY HAVE NINE LIVES!

WHY DO BIRDS FLY SOUTH?
BECAUSE IT'S TOO FAR TO WALK!

ROUND 2 : ANIMAL JOKES

WHY WAS THE CAT SITTING ON THE COMPUTER?
TO KEEP AN EYE ON THE MOUSE!

WHY THE TEDDY BEARS NEVER FEEL HUNGRY?
BECAUSE THEY ARE ALWAYS STUFFED!

WHY DO SEAGULLS LIVE NEAR THE SEA?

BECAUSE IF THEY LIVED NEAR THE BAY, THEY WOULD BE CALLED BAGELS!

WHAT DO YOU GET WHEN YOU CROSS A PARROT WITH A CENTIPEDE?

A WALKIE-TALKIE!

ROUND 2 : ANIMAL JOKES

WHAT DO YOU GIVE A DOG WITH A FEVER?

MUSTARD, ITS THE BEST THING FOR A HOT DOG!

WHAT DO BABY KANGAROOS WEAR WHEN IT'S COLD OUTSIDE?

JUMPSUITS!

ROUND 3

Holiday

Jokes

WHAT KIND OF BIKE DOES SANTA RIDE IN HIS SPARE TIME?

A HOLLY DAVIDSON.

WHAT CAN NEVER EVER BE EATEN FOR THANKSGIVING DINNER?

THANKSGIVING BREAKFAST!

ROUND 3 : HOLIDAY JOKES

WHAT IS A LION'S FAVORITE CHRISTMAS CAROL?

JUNGLE BELLS!

WHY SHOULD YOU NEVER MESS WITH SANTA?

BECAUSE HE'S GOT A BLACK BELT!

WHY SHOULD YOU NEVER IRON A FOUR-LEAF CLOVER?
BECAUSE YOU SHOULDN'T PRESS YOUR LUCK.

WHY DON'T ALIENS CELEBRATE CHRISTMAS?
BECAUSE THEY DON'T WANT TO GIVE AWAY THEIR PRESENCE.

ROUND 3 : HOLIDAY JOKES

WHAT DO SNOWMEN LIKE TO DO ON THE WEEKEND?
CHILL OUT.

WHICH SIDE OF A TURKEY HAS THE MOST FEATHERS?
THE OUTSIDE!

WHY DID THE FARMER WEAR ONE BOOT TO TOWN?
BECAUSE HE HEARD THERE WOULD BE A 50% CHANCE OF SNOW!

WHAT IS A PUMPKIN'S FAVORITE SPORT?
SQUASH!

ROUND 3 : HOLIDAY JOKES

WHY DOES SANTA RIDE A SLEIGH?
IT'S TOO HEAVY TO CARRY!

HOW DID SCROOGE WIN THE FOOTBALL GAME?
THE GHOST OF CHRISTMAS PASSED.

CAN FEBRUARY MARCH?
NO, BUT APRIL MAY.

WHICH OF SANTA'S REINDEER HAS BAD MANNERS?
RUDE-OLPH!

ROUND 3 : HOLIDAY JOKES

HOW DO YOU KNOW CARROTS ARE GOOD FOR YOUR EYES?
HAVE YOU EVER SEEN AN EASTER BUNNY WEARING GLASSES?

WHAT'S A GOOD WINTER TIP?
NEVER CATCH SNOWFLAKES WITH YOUR TONGUE UNTIL ALL THE BIRDS HAVE GONE SOUTH FOR THE WINTER.

WHAT DID ADAM SAY THE DAY BEFORE CHRISTMAS?

IT'S CHRISTMAS EVE!

WHY ARE CHRISTMAS TREES SO BAD AT SEWING?

THEY ALWAYS DROP THEIR NEEDLES!

ROUND 3 : HOLIDAY JOKES

WHY DID THE EASTER BUNNY HAVE TO FIRE THE DUCK?

BECAUSE HE KEPT QUACKING ALL THE EGGS!

WHY DID THE PILGRIMS EAT TURKEY AT THANKSGIVING?

BECAUSE THEY COULDN'T FIT THE MOOSE IN THE OVEN!

WHO IS FROSTY'S FAVORITE AUNT?
AUNT ARCTICA!

WHAT SORTS OF CAKES DO SNOWMEN LIKE BEST?
ONES WITH THICK ICING.

ROUND 3 : HOLIDAY JOKES

WHAT DID THE SNOWMAN SAY TO A KID?
HAVE AN ICE DAY!

WHAT'S THE KEY TO A GREAT THANKSGIVING DINNER?
THE TUR-KEY!

WHY WAS THE SNOWMAN'S DOG CALLED FROST?
BECAUSE FROST BITES!

WHAT DO YOU CALL A SNOWMAN IN THE DESERT?
A PUDDLE!

ROUND 3 : HOLIDAY JOKES

WHAT'S THE BEST TIME FOR SANTA TO COME DOWN THE CHIMNEY?
ANYTIME!

WHAT'S THE DIFFERENCE BETWEEN SANTA'S REINDEER AND A KNIGHT?
ONE SLAYS THE DRAGON, THE OTHER'S DRAGGIN' THE SLEIGH.

WHY DO PUMPKINS SIT ON PEOPLE'S PORCHES?
THEY HAVE NO HANDS TO KNOCK ON THE DOOR.

WHAT NATIONALITY IS SANTA CLAUS?
NORTH POLISH!

ROUND 3 : HOLIDAY JOKES

WHY COULDN'T PREHISTORIC MAN SEND HOLIDAY CARDS?
THE STAMPS KEPT FALLING OFF THE ROCKS!

WHY DOES SANTA GO DOWN THE CHIMNEY ON CHRISTMAS?
BECAUSE IT SOOTS HIM!

WHICH TYPE OF DONUTS DOES SANTA PREFER?
THE ONES WITH THE HO-HO-HOLE.

HOW DOES A SNOWMAN GET TO WORK?
BY ICICLE!

ROUND 3 : HOLIDAY JOKES

WHAT DO YOU CALL PEOPLE WHO ARE AFRAID OF SANTA CLAUS?
CLAUSTROPHOBIC!

WHY YOU SHOULDN'T SEND LETTERS TO SANTA UP THE CHIMNEY?
BECAUSE IT'S A BLACK MAIL!

ROUND 4

Food

Jokes

WHAT KIND OF SHOES DO YOU MAKE FROM BANANAS?
A SLIPPERS!

HOW DO LEMONS ASK FOR A HUG?
"GIVE US A SQUEEZE!"

ROUND 4 : FOOD JOKES

WHAT DAY DO POTATOES HATE?
FRY-DAY!

WHAT DO YOU CALL A BEAR WITH NO TEETH?
A GUMMY BEAR!

WHAT'S THE BEST FOOD WHEN YOU'RE SO HUNGRY YOU COULD EAT A HOUSE?

WALL NUTS, COTTAGE CHEESE, AND KITCHEN SINK COOKIES.

WHAT DO YOU CALL BLUEBERRIES PLAYING THE GUITAR?

A JAM SESSION.

ROUND 4 : FOOD JOKES

WHAT'S THE BEST FOOD TO EAT BEFORE A WORKOUT?

MUSSELS!

WHAT SHOULD YOU DO IF YOUR SOUP IS TOO HOT?

ADD A CHILLY PEPPER!

WHAT DO YOU GET WHEN YOU CROSS A COMPUTER WITH A HAMBURGER?

A BIG MAC!

IF YOU DIVIDE AN ORANGE BETWEEN FIVE FRIENDS, WHAT DO THEY EACH GET?

STICKY FINGERS!

ROUND 4 : FOOD JOKES

WHY SHOULDN'T YOU TELL SECRETS ON A FARM?

BECAUSE THE POTATOES HAVE EYES, THE CORN HAS EARS, AND THE BEANS STALK.

WHAT DO YOU CALL A MONKEY WITH A BANANA IN EACH EAR?

YOU CAN CALL IT WHATEVER YOU WANT, IT CAN'T HEAR YOU!

WHEN DOES AN ASTRONAUT EAT HIS FAVOURITE MEAL?
AT LAUNCH!

WHY DID THE DONUT GO TO THE DENTIST?
HE NEEDED A CHOCOLATE FILLING.

ROUND 4 : FOOD JOKES

WHAT IS FAST FOOD?
A CHICKEN RUNNING DOWN THE ROAD.

WHY WAS THE CUCUMBER MAD?
BECAUSE IT WAS IN A PICKLE!

WHAT IS THE MOST MYSTERIOUS VEGETABLE?

THE UNICORN.

HOW DO YOU CALL A FAKE NOODLE?

AN IMPASTA!

ROUND 4 : FOOD JOKES

WHAT DID ONE PLATE SAY TO ANOTHER?

LUNCH IS ON ME!

WHAT DOES A NUT SAY WHEN IT SNEEZES?

CASHEW!

DO YOU WANT TO HEAR A JOKE ABOUT PIZZA?
NEVER MIND, IT'S TOO CHEESY.

WHAT IS DRACULA'S FAVORITE FRUIT?
NECK-TARINES.

ROUND 4 : FOOD JOKES

WHAT DO YOU GET WHEN YOU MIX LEMONS WITH GUNPOWDER?
LEMONADES.

WHAT IS IT CALLED WHEN YOU PUT A COW IN AN ELEVATOR?
RAISING THE STEAKS.

WHY DID THE FRENCH FRY WIN THE RACE?
BECAUSE IT WAS FAST FOOD!

WAITER, WILL MY PIZZA BE LONG?
NO, IT WILL BE ROUND.

ROUND 4 : FOOD JOKES

WHAT'S THE WORST THING ABOUT BEING AN OCTOPUS?
WASHING YOUR HANDS BEFORE BREAKFAST.

WHY DID THE BAKER STOP MAKING DOUGHNUTS?
BECAUSE SHE WAS BORED WITH THE HOLE BUSINESS!

WHY WAS THE POTATO SUCH A BULLY?
BECAUSE IT WASN'T A SWEET POTATO.

WHY DID THE TOMATO TURN RED?
BECAUSE IT SAW THE SALAD DRESSING!

ROUND 4 : FOOD JOKES

WHY WAS THE BOY STARING AT THE CAN OF ORANGE JUICE?
BECAUSE IT SAID "CONCENTRATE".

WHY DID THE MAN CLIMB ON THE ROOF OF THE RESTAURANT?
BECAUSE THE WAITER TOLD HIM THE MEAL WAS ON THE HOUSE.

HOW CAN YOU FIX A BROKEN TOMATO?
WITH TOMATO PASTE!

WHAT DID THE PEPPERONI SAY TO THE COOK?
DO YOU WANNA PIZZA ME?!

ROUND 4 : FOOD JOKES

WHY DID THE COOKIE GO TO THE DOCTOR?
BECAUSE IT WAS FEELING CRUMMY!

WHY DID THE GRAPE STOP RUNNING DOWN THE ROAD?
BECAUSE HE RAN OUT OF JUICE.

WHAT FOOD IS GOOD FOR YOUR BRAIN?

NOODLE SOUP!

WHERE DO BURGERS GO DANCING?

TO A MEAT BALL!

ROUND 4 : FOOD JOKES

WHAT DO YOU GIVE TO A SICK LEMON?

LEMON AID!

WHY DID THE STUDENT EAT HIS HOMEWORK?

THE TEACHER TOLD HIM IT WAS A PIECE OF CAKE.

ROUND 5

Nature&Geography

Jokes

WHAT DID DELAWARE?
A NEW JERSEY.

WHICH ROCK BAND HAS FOUR MEN THAT DON'T SING?
MOUNT RUSHMORE!

ROUND 5 : NATURE & GEOGRAPHY

WHAT IS A TORNADO'S FAVORITE GAME?
TWISTER!

WHO WAS MISSISSIPPI MARRIED TOO?
MISTER SIPPI!

DID YOU HEAR ABOUT ITALY?

IT GOT HUNGARY, ATE TURKEY, WENT SHOPPING IN ICELAND, SLIPPED ON GREECE, AND THEN GOT EATEN BY WALES.

IF YOU PUT A GREEN ROCK IN THE RED SEA, WHAT WILL HAPPEN?

IT WILL GET WET!

ROUND 5 : NATURE & GEOGRAPHY

WHAT IS THE BIGGEST COW IN THE WORLD THAT DOESN'T GIVE ANY MILK?

MOS-COW!

TEACHER: WHAT CAN YOU TELL US ABOUT THE DEAD SEA?

STUDENT: I DIDN'T EVEN KNOW IT WAS SICK!

WHAT IS THE HAPPIEST STATE IN THE USA?
MERRY-LAND!

WHAT IS THE BIGGEST PAN IN THE WORLD?
JA-PAN!

ROUND 5 : NATURE & GEOGRAPHY

HOW CAN YOU TELL THAT COMPASSES AND SCALES ARE INTELLIGENT?
BECAUSE THEY ALL GRADUATED.

WHAT IS THE DIFFERENCE BETWEEN A HORSE AND THE WEATHER?
ONE IS REINED UP AND THE OTHER RAINS DOWN!

WHY DON'T YOU SEE PENGUINS IN GREAT BRITAIN?
BECAUSE THEY'RE AFRAID OF WALES.

WHAT WASHES UP ON SMALL BEACHES?
MICROWAVES!

ROUND 5 : NATURE & GEOGRAPHY

WHAT DID THE TORNADO SAY TO A CAR?
WANT TO GO FOR A SPIN!

WHICH COUNTRY IS THE FASTEST?
RUSH-A!

WHICH MEMBER OF THE ORCHESTRA IS MOST LIKELY TO GET HIT BY LIGHTNING?

THE CONDUCTOR!

WHY DO PEOPLE WEAR SHAMROCKS ON ST. PATRICK'S DAY?

REAL ROCKS ARE VERY HEAVY!

ROUND 5 : NATURE & GEOGRAPHY

WHAT KIND OF PUDDING ROAMS IN THE ARCTIC CIRCLE?

MOOSE.

HOW DID CHRISTOPHER COLUMBUS PAY FOR HIS TRIP TO THE NEW LAND?

HE USED HIS DISCOVER CARD.

WHEN IS THE MOON THE HEAVIEST?
WHEN IT'S FULL!

WHAT DID MARS SAY TO SATURN?
GIVE ME A RING SOMETIME.

ROUND 5 : NATURE & GEOGRAPHY

WHY DID THE MAP ALWAYS GET IN TROUBLE?
IT HAD BAD LATITUDE.

WHAT KIND OF TREE YOU CAN PLACE IN YOUR HAND?
A PALM TREE!

WHAT IS THE BIGGEST MARK IN THE WORLD?
DEN-MARK!

HOW DO TREES GET ON THE INTERNET?
THEY LOG IN.

ROUND 5 : NATURE & GEOGRAPHY

WHAT KIND OF FLOWERS GROW ON YOUR FACE?
TULIPS!

WHAT DID THE GROUND SAY TO THE EARTHQUAKE?
"YOU CRACK ME UP!"

WHERE IS THE ENGLISH CHANNEL?
IT DEPENDS ON WHO IS YOUR CABLE PROVIDER.

WHAT IS THE OPPOSITE OF A COLD FRONT?
A WARM BACK!

ROUND 5 : NATURE & GEOGRAPHY

WHAT TYPE OF LIGHTNING LIKES TO PLAY SOCCER?
BALL LIGHTNING!

WHAT KIND OF SONGS DO THE PLANETS SING?
NEP-TUNES!

WHAT IS SMARTER, LATITUDE OR LONGITUDE?
LONGITUDE, BECAUSE IT HAS 360 DEGREES.

WHAT DID ONE PYRAMID SAY TO THE OTHER?
HOW'S YOUR MUMMY DOING?

ROUND 5 : NATURE & GEOGRAPHY

WHAT DID THE BIG FLOWER SAY TO THE SMALL FLOWER?
"WHAT'S UP, BUD?"

WHAT DID THE SMALL ROCK SAY TO THE BIG ROCK?
I WISH I WERE BOULDER!

ROUND 6

Sports

Jokes

WHY DO SOME FOOTBALL PLAYERS NEVER SWEAT?
BECAUSE OF ALL THE FANS!

WHY WAS THE SOCCER FIELD WET ON A SUNNY DAY?
BECAUSE THE PLAYERS DRIBBLED ALL OVER IT.

ROUND 6 : SPORTS JOKES

WHY CAN'T CINDERELLA PLAY BASKETBALL?
BECAUSE SHE IS ALWAYS RUNNING AWAY FROM THE BALL.

WHY DO BASKETBALL PLAYERS LOVE COOKIES?
BECAUSE THEY CAN DUNK THEM.

WHAT'S THE DIFFERENCE BETWEEN A QUARTERBACK AND A NEWBORN BABY?

ONE TAKES THE SNAP, THE OTHER TAKES A NAP.

WHAT SHOULD YOU DO IF YOU SEE AN ELEPHANT PLAYING BASKETBALL?

GET OUT OF THE WAY!

ROUND 6 : SPORTS JOKES

WHAT DID THE ARCHER GET WHEN HE HIT A BULLSEYE?

A VERY ANGRY BULL.

WHAT HAS EIGHTEEN LEGS AND CATCHES FLIES?

A BASEBALL TEAM!

WHY DID THE SOCCER BALL QUIT THE GAME?
IT WAS TIRED OF BEING KICKED AROUND.

WHAT DID THE BASEBALL GLOVE SAY TO THE BALL?
"CATCH YA LATER!"

ROUND 6 : SPORTS JOKES

WHICH BASEBALL PLAYER HOLDS WATER?
THE PITCHER.

HOW DO YOU MAKE A FRUIT PUNCH?
GIVE IT BOXING LESSONS.

WHY DO FIGURE SKATERS WORK IN BAKERIES WHEN THEY RETIRE?

THEY ARE GREAT AT ICING CAKES.

WHICH FIGURE SKATER CAN JUMP HIGHER THAN THE JUDGE'S TABLE?

ANY. A TABLE CAN'T JUMP.

ROUND 6 : SPORTS JOKES

WHY CAN'T YOU PLAY A FAIR BASKETBALL GAME IN THE JUNGLE?

TOO MANY CHEETAHS.

WHAT HAS A SPIKED TAIL, PLATES ON ITS BACK, AND 16 WHEELS?

A DINOSAUR ON ROLLER SKATES!

WHY DID THE BASKETBALL PLAYER GO TO JAIL?

BECAUSE HE SHOT THE BALL!

WHAT DO HOCKEY PLAYER AND MAGICIAN HAVE IN COMMON?

THEY BOTH DO HAT TRICKS!

ROUND 6 : SPORTS JOKES

HOW IS A BASEBALL TEAM SIMILAR TO A PANCAKE?

THEY BOTH NEED A GOOD BATTER.

WHY WAS CINDERELLA SUCH A BAD BOWLER?

HER COACH WAS A PUMPKIN.

WHY ARE SPIDERS GOOD AT BASEBALL?

BECAUSE THEY KNOW HOW TO CATCH FLIES!

WHY SHOULD A BOWLING ALLEY BE QUIET?

SO YOU CAN HEAR A PIN DROP!

ROUND 6 : SPORTS JOKES

HOW DID THE FOOTBALL GROUND END UP IN A TRIANGLE?

SOMEONE TOOK A CORNER!

WHY CAN'T YOU TELL A JOKE WHILE DOING ICE SKATING?

BECAUSE THE ICE MIGHT CRACK UP.

WHAT IS THE HARDEST IN SKYDIVING?
THE GROUND!

WHY DIDN'T THE DOG WANT TO PLAY FOOTBALL?
BECAUSE IT WAS A BOXER!

ROUND 6 : SPORTS JOKES

WHAT KIND OF STORIES DO BASKETBALL PLAYERS TELL?
TALL TALES.

WHAT IS A BOXER'S FAVORITE PART OF A JOKE?
THE PUNCH-LINE!

HY WAS THE TINY GHOST ASKED TO JOIN THE FOOTBALL TEAM?

THEY NEEDED A LITTLE TEAM SPIRIT.

WHICH FAST FOOD CHAIN IS MOST LIKELY TO WIN A BASKETBALL TOURNAMENT?

DUNKIN' DONUTS!

ROUND 6 : SPORTS JOKES

WHY ARE BASEBALL GAMES PLAYED AT NIGHT?

THE BATS SLEEP DURING THE DAY.

WHY DID THE FOOTBALL COACH GO TO THE BANK?

TO GET HIS QUARTER BACK.

WHY CAN'T YOU PLAY SOCCER WITH PIGS?
THEY HOG THE BALL.

WHAT IS BUG'S FAVORITE SPORT?
CRICKET!

ROUND 6 : SPORTS JOKES

WHAT KIND OF BOW CANNOT BE TIED?
A RAINBOW!

WHEN SHOULD FOOTBALL PLAYERS WEAR ARMOR?
WHEN THEY PLAY KNIGHT GAMES.

ROUND 7

school

jokes

WHAT WOULD YOU GET IF YOU CROSSED A TEACHER AND A VAMPIRE?

LOTS OF BLOOD TESTS!

WHAT DO YOU CALL A BOY WITH A DICTIONARY IN HIS POCKET?

SMARTIE PANTS!

ROUND 7 : SCHOOL JOKES

WHY DID THE STUDENT THROW HIS WATCH OUT OF THE SCHOOL WINDOW?

HE WANTED TO SEE TIME FLY.

WHAT DID THE CALCULATOR SAY TO THE OTHER CALCULATOR?

"YOU CAN COUNT ON ME!"

HOW DO YOU GET STRAIGHT A'S?
BY USING A RULER!

WHY DIDN'T THE SUN GO TO COLLEGE?
BECAUSE IT ALREADY HAD A MILLION DEGREES.

ROUND 7 : SCHOOL JOKES

WHY WAS 6 AFRAID OF 7?
BECAUSE 7 8 9.

HOW DO YOU SPELL HARD WATER WITH 3 LETTERS?
ICE!

WHAT FLIES AROUND THE SCHOOL AT NIGHT?
THE ALPHA-BAT.

WHY DID THE CYCLOPS STOP TEACHING?
BECAUSE HE ONLY HAD ONE PUPIL.

ROUND 7 : SCHOOL JOKES

WHY WAS THE STUDENT'S REPORT CARD WET?
BECAUSE IT WAS BELOW C LEVEL.

WHY WAS THE MATH BOOK SAD?
BECAUSE IT HAD TOO MANY PROBLEMS.

WHY DID THE TEACHER WEAR SUNGLASSES?
BECAUSE HER STUDENTS WERE VERY BRIGHT!

WHAT IS THE SMARTEST STATE?
ALABAMA, IT HAS FOUR A'S AND ONE B!

ROUND 7 : SCHOOL JOKES

WHY DID THE NEW BOY STEAL A CHAIR FROM THE CLASSROOM?
BECAUSE THE TEACHER TOLD HIM TO TAKE A SEAT.

WHAT HAS GIVEN MR.BUBBLES NIGHTMARES SINCE ELEMENTARY SCHOOL?
POP QUIZZES!

WHAT KIND OF FOOD DO MATH TEACHERS EAT?
SQUARE MEALS!

WHY DID THE MUSIC TEACHER NEED A LADDER?
TO REACH THE HIGH NOTES.

ROUND 7 : SCHOOL JOKES

WHAT DID THE SQUARE SAY TO THE OLD CIRCLE?
BEEN AROUND LONG?

WHAT HAPPENED TO THE PLANT IN MATH CLASS?
IT GREW SQUARE ROOTS!

WHY IS 2+2:5 LIKE YOUR LEFT FOOT?

IT'S NOT RIGHT!

WHY WAS SCHOOL MUCH EASIER FOR CAVE PEOPLE?

BECAUSE THERE WAS NO HISTORY LESSONS!

ROUND 7 : SCHOOL JOKES

WHY DID THE BOY TAKE A LADDER TO SCHOOL?

BECAUSE HE THOUGHT IT WAS A HIGH SCHOOL!

WHO IS YOUR BEST FRIEND AT SCHOOL?

PRINCI-PAL!

WHY WERE THE TEACHER'S EYES CROSSED?
SHE COULDN'T CONTROL HER PUPILS.

WHAT TOOLS DO YOU NEED FOR MATH?
MULTI-PLIERS!

ROUND 7 : SCHOOL JOKES

WHAT KIND OF SCHOOL DO YOU GO TO IF YOU'RE A SURFER?
BOARDING SCHOOL!

WHAT KIND OF SCHOOL DO YOU GO TO IF YOU'RE AN ICE CREAM MAN?
SUNDAE SCHOOL!

WHAT HAPPENED WHEN THE TEACHER TIED ALL THE KIDS SHOE LACES TOGETHER?

THEY HAD A CLASS TRIP!

WHAT IS YELLOW ON THE OUTSIDE AND GRAY ON THE INSIDE?

A SCHOOL BUS FULL OF ELEPHANTS!

ROUND 7 : SCHOOL JOKES

WHAT DO YOU GET WHEN YOU CROSS A TEACHER WITH A TIGER?

I DON'T KNOW BUT YOU BETTER BEHAVE IN ITS CLASS!

WHAT DID THE STUDENT SAY AFTER THE TEACHER SAID, "ORDER STUDENTS, ORDER?"

"CAN I HAVE FRIES AND A BURGER?"

WHY WAS THE VOICE TEACHER SO GOOD AT BASEBALL?

BECAUSE SHE HAD THE PERFECT PITCH.

WHY DID THE TEACHER WRITE THE LESSON ON THE WINDOWS?

HE WANTED THE LESSON TO BE VERY CLEAR!

ROUND 7 : SCHOOL JOKES

WHERE ARE THE GREAT PLAINS LOCATED?

AT THE GREAT AIRPORTS!

WHY DID THE KID RUN TO SCHOOL?

BECAUSE HE WAS CHASED BY THE SPELLING BEE!

WHY DOES NOBODY TALK TO CIRCLES?
BECAUSE THERE IS NO POINT!

HOW DO YOU SPELL MOUSETRAP?
C-A-T

ROUND 7 : SCHOOL JOKES

TEACHER: WHY IS YOUR HOMEWORK IN YOUR FATHER'S HANDWRITING?
PUPIL: I USED HIS PEN!

WHAT'S A TEACHER'S FAVORITE NATION?
EXPLA-NATION.

ROUND 8

Jokes About

Everything

WHAT DID THE TRAFFIC LIGHT SAY TO THE CAR?
DON'T LOOK NOW. I'M CHANGING!

WHY DID THE BARBER WIN THE RACE?
BECAUSE HE KNEW A SHORTCUT.

ROUND 8: JOKES ABOUT EVERYTHING

WHY DID THE COMPUTER GO TO THE DENTIST?
BECAUSE IT HAD BLUETOOTH.

WHAT KIND OF SHOES DO SPIES WEAR?
SNEAKERS.

WHAT GIVES YOU THE POWER AND STRENGTH TO WALK THROUGH WALLS?

A DOOR!

WHAT IS THE MOST DANGEROUS JOB IN TRANSYLVANIA?

DRACULA'S DENTIST.

ROUND 8: JOKES ABOUT EVERYTHING

WHAT IS YELLOW, BIG AND COMES EVERY MORNING TO BRIGHTEN MOM'S DAY?

SCHOOL BUS!

WHAT'S THE DIFFERENCE BETWEEN A NEWSPAPER AND A TV?

HAVE YOU EVER TRIED SWATTING A FLY WITH A TV?

WHY DID THE INVISIBLE MAN QUIT THE JOB?
HE COULDN'T SEE HIMSELF DOING IT.

WHY DID THE THIEF TAKE A SHOWER?
HE WANTED TO MAKE A CLEAN GETAWAY!

ROUND 8: JOKES ABOUT EVERYTHING

WHERE ARE CARS MOST LIKELY TO GET FLAT TIRES?
AT FORKS IN THE ROAD!

HOW DO YOU MAKE AN EGG ROLL?
YOU PUSH IT!

WHY DID THE FARMER BURY ALL HIS MONEY?
TO MAKE HIS SOIL RICH!

WHAT DID ONE EYE SAY TO THE OTHER?
BETWEEN YOU AND ME SOMETHING SMELLS.

ROUND 8: JOKES ABOUT EVERYTHING

WHAT DID THE OLDER CHIMNEY SAY TO THE YOUNGER ONE?
YOU'RE WAY TOO YOUNG TO SMOKE!

WHAT DO YOU CALL SOMEONE WITH NO BODY AND NO NOSE?
NOBODY KNOWS!

WHAT HAS FORTY FEET AND CAN SING?
THE SCHOOL CHOIR!

WHAT ANIMAL IS ALWAYS LOST?
A WHERE WOLF!

ROUND 8: JOKES ABOUT EVERYTHING

WHAT NAILS DOES CARPENTER HATE TO HIT?
FINGERNAILS!

WHAT HAS FOUR WHEELS AND FLIES?
A GARBAGE TRUCK!

WHICH ARE THE STRONGER DAYS OF THE WEEK?
SATURDAY AND SUNDAY. THE REST ARE WEAK-DAYS.

WHAT IS THE BEST THING TO PUT INTO A PIE?
A FORK!

ROUND 8: JOKES ABOUT EVERYTHING

WHY DID THE RUNNER STOP LISTENING TO MUSIC?
BECAUSE SHE BROKE TOO MANY RECORDS.

WHAT KIND OF BUTTON CAN YOU NOT UNDO?
A BELLY BUTTON!

WHY DID THE MAN THROW THE BUTTER OUT THE WINDOW?

BECAUSE HE WANTED TO SEE BUTTER-FLY.

WHY CAN'T YOU PLAY HIDE-AND-SEEK WITH MOUNTAINS?

BECAUSE THEY'RE ALWAYS PEAKING.

ROUND 8: JOKES ABOUT EVERYTHING

WHICH WORD IS SPELLED INCORRECTLY IN THE DICTIONARY?

INCORRECTLY!

WHAT DO YOU CALL A BOOMERANG THAT DOESN'T COME BACK?

A STICK!

WHAT KIND OF A STAR CAN BE DANGEROUS?
A SHOOTING STAR!

WHAT DID ONE HAT SAY TO THE OTHER?
YOU STAY HERE. I'LL GO ON AHEAD.

ROUND 8: JOKES ABOUT EVERYTHING

WHY CAN'T YOU TRUST ATOMS?
THEY MAKE UP EVERYTHING!

WHAT'S RED AND BAD FOR YOUR TEETH?
A BRICK.

WHAT DID THE TIE SAY TO A HAT?
YOU GO ON AHEAD AND I'LL HANG AROUND.

WHY WAS BABY ANT CONFUSED?
BECAUSE ALL HIS UNCLES WERE ANTS!

ROUND 8: JOKES ABOUT EVERYTHING

WHAT DO YOU DO WITH A SICK BOAT?
TAKE IT TO THE DOC IMMEDIATELY!

WHAT IS BROWN, HAIRY AND WEARS SUNGLASSES?
A COCONUT ON VACATION.

DID YOU HEAR ABOUT THE KIDNAPPING AT SCHOOL?

IT'S ALL RIGHT, HE WOKE UP.

WHAT'S THE MOST FAMOUS FISH IN THE OCEAN?

A STARFISH!

ROUND 8: JOKES ABOUT EVERYTHING

WHAT DOES AN ENVELOPE SAY WHEN YOU LICK IT?

NOTHING. IT JUST SHUTS UP.

HOW DO YOU TALK TO A GIANT?

USE BIG WORDS!

WHY WAS THE BOY SITTING ON HIS WATCH?
BECAUSE HE WANTED TO BE ON TIME.

HOW DOES A SCIENTIST FRESHEN HER BREATH?
WITH EXPERI-MINTS!

ROUND 8: JOKES ABOUT EVERYTHING

WHAT IS THE COLOR OF THE WIND?
BLEW!

WHY DID THE BANANA GO TO THE DOCTOR?
BECAUSE HE WASN'T PEELING VERY WELL!

WHAT DID THE BABY CORN SAY TO A MAMA CORN?

WHERE IS POPCORN?

WHAT DID THE BLANKET SAY TO THE BED?

DON'T WORRY. I GOT YOU COVERED.

ROUND 8: JOKES ABOUT EVERYTHING

WHAT DID THE PICTURE SAY TO THE WALL?

I WAS FRAMED!

WHO DOES A PHARAOH TALK TO WHEN HE'S SAD?

HIS MUMMY, OF COURSE.

WHAT KIND OF DRIVER NEEDS NO LICENSE?
SCREWDRIVER!

WHY DID THE SKELETON GO TO THE PIANO STORE?
TO BUY ORGANS!

ROUND 8: JOKES ABOUT EVERYTHING

WHY IS PETER PAN ALWAYS FLYING?
HE NEVERLANDS!

WHY WAS THE BROOM LATE?
IT OVER SWEPT!

WHAT'S BLACK AND WHITE AND MAKES A LOUD NOISE?
A ZEBRA WITH A DRUM KIT!

WHAT'S THE HOTTEST PART OF A ROOM?
THE CORNER, IT IS 90 DEGREES.

ROUND 8: JOKES ABOUT EVERYTHING

WHAT DO YOU CALL SECURITY GUARDS IN A SAMSUNG STORE?
GUARDIANS OF THE GALAXY!

WHY DO WE PUT CANDLES ON TOP OF A BIRTHDAY CAKE?
BECAUSE IT'S TOO HARD TO PUT THEM ON THE BOTTOM!

WHY DID TIGGER STICK HIS HEAD IN THE TOILET?

BECAUSE HE WAS LOOKING FOR POOH!

WHAT DID THE LIMESTONE SAY TO THE GEOLOGIST?

DON'T TAKE ME FOR GRANITE!

ROUND 8: JOKES ABOUT EVERYTHING

WHAT TIME IS IT WHEN A HIPPO SITS ON YOUR FENCE?

TIME TO BUY A NEW FENCE.

WHAT KIND OF MUSIC IS BALLOON SCARED OF?

POP MUSIC!

WHY DID THE MAN RUN AROUND THE BED?
HE WANTED TO CATCH UP ON HIS SLEEP!

WHY DID THE BOY BURY HIS FLASHLIGHT?
BECAUSE THE BATTERIES WERE DEAD.

ROUND 8: JOKES ABOUT EVERYTHING

WHY DID THE MELON JUMP INTO THE LAKE?
IT WANTED TO BE A WATERMELON!

WHAT DO YOU CALL A FLY WITHOUT WINGS?
A WALK!

WHAT ROOM IS USELESS FOR ZOMBIES?
A LIVING ROOM!

WHY DID MICKEY MOUSE GO INTO SPACE?
HE WANTED TO FIND PLUTO!

ROUND 8: JOKES ABOUT EVERYTHING

WHAT IS FAST, LOUD AND CRUNCHY?
A ROCKET CHIP!

WHAT'S THE BIGGEST MOUSE IN THE WORLD?
HIPPOPOTAMOUSE.

WHY IS IT IMPOSSIBLE FOR YOUR NOSE TO BE 12 INCHES LONG?

BECAUSE THEN IT WOULD BECOME A FOOT!

WHY WAS THE KNIGHT RUNNING AROUND, YELLING FOR A TIN OPENER?

THERE WAS A BEE IN HIS SUIT OF ARMOR!

ROUND 8: JOKES ABOUT EVERYTHING

WHAT DO YOU GET IF YOU CROSS AN INSECT WITH A CUTE EASTER RABBIT?

BUGS BUNNY!

WHAT DOES A SNAIL SAY WHEN HE FINDS HIMSELF ON A TURTLE'S BACK?

WHEEEE!!!

YOUR REVIEW

I HOPE YOU'VE ENJOYED READING THIS LITTLE BOOK. AND IT WOULD BE GREAT IF YOU COULD TAKE A MOMENT OF YOUR TIME TO WRITE DOWN A SHORT REVIEW ON THE BOOK'S AMAZON PAGE. YOUR FEEDBACK IS VERY IMPORTANT TO ME. IT WILL ALSO HELP OTHERS TO MAKE AN INFORMED DECISION BEFORE PURCHASING THIS BOOK. THANK YOU IN ADVANCE.

- DAN GILDEN

Printed in the USA
CPSIA information can be obtained
at www.ICGtesting.com
LVHW020217051223
765723LV00013B/786